# Illinois' Medical Marijuana Law FAQ Handbook
*Part of the eBook Esquire Series*

*By Cameron R. Monti, Esq.*

**DISCLAIMER**

You should not act based upon any information in this Illinois' Medical Marijuana Law FAQ Handbook without first seeking professional legal or tax counsel. *The information presented in this Illinois' Medical Marijuana Law FAQ Handbook is intended to be for informational purposes only and should not be construed to be formal legal advice or the formation of a lawyer or attorney-client relationship*.

## ABOUT THE AUTHOR

Cameron R. Monti is a Partner at the Illinois (Chicago and Palatine) law firm, Lavelle Law, Ltd. Cameron's law practice primarily focuses on the areas of tax law, corporate law, and employment law. Cameron serves as an adjunct professor of law at John Marshall Law School (Chicago) teaching classes in the area of federal tax practice and procedure. In 2001, Cameron earned his law degree from Michigan State University College of Law, and in 2002, received his LL.M. (Master of Laws) in Taxation Law from the University of Washington School of Law in Seattle, WA. Cameron currently resides in the Northwest suburbs of Illinois with his wife, Roxanne, and two boys, Caden and Colsten.

# Illinois' Medical Marijuana Law FAQ Handbook
## TABLE OF CONTENTS / INDEX

**INTRODUCTION**
Purpose of the marijuana law   1-100
Effective date of marijuana law   1-101
Other jurisdictions with similar law   1-102
Pilot program   1-103

**MEDICAL MARIJUANA PATIENTS / DESIGNATED CAREGIVERS**
Government regulatory agencies   2-100
Eligibility to be a patient user/designated caregiver   2-101
Registry identification cards   2-102
Application Process / requirements   2-103
Application approval or denial time   2-104
Grounds for denial of application (patient user)   2-105
Grounds for denial of application (designated caregiver)   2-106
Issuance of registration card time period   2-107
Failure to approve or deny application   2-108
Appeal rights upon denial of application   2-109
Length of time /expiration of registration card   2-110
Notice requirements for registry card   2-111
Amount of medical marijuana   2-112
Authorized higher amounts of medical marijuana   2-113
Tax on use of medical marijuana   2-114
Medical conditions that qualify for medical marijuana use   2-115
Medical conditions not in Act for medical marijuana use   2-116
Health insurance reimbursement   2-117
Change of designated caregiver   2-118
 Lost registry ID card   2-119
Other compliance obligations as a patient user   2-220
Other compliance obligations as a designated caregiver   2-221

**EMPLOYER/EMPLOYEE LEGAL ISSUES**
Employment rules and restrictions   3-100
Disciplinary action against employee for user status   3-101
Drug testing / zero tolerance policies   3-102
Disciplinary action against employee violating policy   3-103
Disciplinary action against employee for failed drug test   3-104
Defense by third party   3-105

Impairment from medical marijuana use   3-106
Right of employee to contest employer disciplinary action   3-107
Liability for wrongfully accusing employee of impairment   3-108
Third party liability against employer   3-109
Prohibited medical marijuana use for certain jobs   3-110
Inter-agency reporting of offenses   3-111
Unlawful disclosure of private information by agency   3-112

## HEALTH LAW / PHYSICIAN/ HEALTHCARE PROVIDER ISSUES
Physician liability   4-100
Physician qualifications to certify medical condition   4-101
Certification protocol for debilitating medical condition   4-102
Use of medical marijuana in healthcare facility   4-103
Denial of medical care for patient user status   4-104

## BUSINESS LAW / BUSINESS ENTREPRENUER ISSUES
REGISTERED CULTIVATION CENTERS
Definition of a cultivation center   5-101
Cultivation center agent   5-102
Oversight of cultivation centers   5-103
**Application for Registration Certification**
Basic requirements for cultivation center certification   5-104
Application process   5-105
Time expectancy for application process   5-106
Grounds for denied application   5-107
Application for certification renewal   5-108
Compliance requirements of agents   5-109
**Cultivation Center Facility Compliance**
Regulatory compliance for cultivation facilities   5-110
Inspections   5-111
Privilege Tax   5-112
Tax filing requirements   5-113
Failure to comply with tax obligations   5-114
**Medical Marijuana Products**
Oversight of marijuana food products   5-115
Prohibited marijuana food products   5-116
Product regulations   5-117
**Violations by Cultivation Center**
Public health hazards   5-118
Consequences for violations   5-119

REGISTERED DISPENSING ORGANIZATIONS
Definition of dispensing organization   5-120
Dispensing agents   5-121
Oversight of dispensing organizations   5-122
**Application for Registration**
Basic requirements for dispensing organization   5-123
Application process   5-124
Time expectancy for application process   5-125
Grounds for denied application   5-12
Post-application approval compliance   5-127
Application for certification renewal   5-128
Failure to reapply for renewal certification   5-129
**Dispensing Organization Facility Compliance**   5-130
Inspections of facility   5-131
**Dispensing Organization Retail Sales Compliance**   5-132
Retail sales rules and regulations   5-133
Fulfillment of prescriptions   5-134
Medical marijuana food products   5-135
Supermarkets and right to sell products   5-136
Tax on marijuana product sales   5-137
**Violations of Dispensing Organizations**
Violation and consequences   5-138

EDUCATION LAW
Restriction by colleges and universities   6-100
Refusal for admission   6-101

**VIOLATION / SUSPENSIONS / REVOCATIONS OF REGISTRATION**
Violations by cultivation center   7-100
Violations by dispensing organizations   7-101

CRIMINAL LAW
Registered patient information by law enforcement   8-100
Possession of more than legal amount   8-101
Reasonable suspicion or probable cause to search   8-102
In the presence of a patient user   8-103
Illegal areas to possess or use medical marijuana   8-104
Criminal penalties for violations   8-105
DUI of medical marijuana   8-106
Misrepresentation to law enforcement   8-107

Fraud to obtain certification from physician   8-108
Unlawful sale of medical marijuana   8-109
Field sobriety tests   8-110
Prior offenses and convictions   8-111
Unlawful disclosure of private information   8-112
Risk of violating federal criminal law   8-113.

## PROFESSIONAL DISCIPLINARY ACTION
Disciplinary action for being in the presence of a user   9-100
Disciplinary action against physicians -certifications   9-101
Use or possession as a registered user   9-102

## LANDLORD –TENANT LAW
Prohibiting use on premises   10-100

## CIVIL RIGHTS/CONCERN CITIZENS
Denial of medical care   11-100
Accommodations for medical marijuana use   11-101
Complaints against cultivation centers   11-102
Police and government agency inspections   11-103
Privacy concerns   11-104

## FAMILY LAW
Custody and visitation   12-100

# INTRODUCTION

## 1-100. What is the purpose of Illinois' Medical Marijuana Law?

Illinois' Compassionate Use of Medical Cannabis Pilot Program (commonly referred to and referred throughout this Handbook as the **"Medical Marijuana Law"** or **"Law"** or **"Act"**) was passed by the Illinois legislature and signed into law by Governor Pat Quinn to protect patients with debilitating medical conditions, as well as their physicians and providers, from arrest and prosecution, criminal and other penalties, and property forfeiture if the patients engage in the medical use of cannabis [410 ILCS 130/5(g)]. Throughout this Handbook, the terms "marijuana" and "cannabis" are used interchangeably.

## 1-101. When does/did Illinois' Medical Marijuana Law go into effect?

Illinois' Medical Marijuana Law goes/went into effect on January 1, 2014 [410 ILCS 130/5(e)]. Not later than 120 days after the effective date of the Act, the IDPH, IDA, and the IDFRP must develop rules in accordance to their responsibilities under the Act and file those rules with the Joint Committee on Administrative Rules[410 ILCS 130/165(a)]. Within 180 days, the departments must implement a registration verification system.

## 1-102. How many other states have a similar Medical Marijuana Law?

As of 2013, 18 other states and Washington D.C. have a similar medical marijuana law [410 ILCS 130/5(e)]. Therefore, there are currently 20 jurisdictions.

## 1-103. Why is the Act referred to as a "Pilot Program"?

It is referred to as a "Pilot Program" because the law is scheduled to terminate on December 31, 2017, unless the Illinois legislature agrees to extend the law.

# MEDICAL MARIJUANA PATIENTS / DESIGNATED CAREGIVERS

## 2-100. Which Illinois government agencies are involved with the regulation, administration, inspection, supervision, oversight, enforcement of Illinois' Medical Marijuana Law?

The Illinois Department of Public Health (**IDPH**), Illinois Department of Agriculture (**IDA**), the Illinois Department of Financial and Professional Regulation (**IDFPR**) and Illinois State Police are involved with different roles and responsibilities for the regulation, administration, inspection, supervision, oversight, enforcement of Illinois' Medical Marijuana Law.

## 2-101. Who is eligible to apply for a registry card identification card for medical marijuana use?

A patient who is at least age 18-years-old [410 ILCS 130/60(b)], suffers from a debilitating medical condition [410 ILCS 130/10(h)(1)], and seeks the use and relief of medical marijuana, as a qualifying patient, to alleviate or treat the patient's debilitating medical condition [410 ILCS 130/5(b)], or a designated caregiver who is at least 21-years-old and has agreed to assist with a patient's medical use of marijuana [410 ILCS 130/10(i)]. Those persons who are issued and possess registry identification cards by the IDPH are referred to as "cardholders" under the Law [410 ILCS 130/10(d)].

## 2-102. How does a patient or designated caregiver of a patient go about obtaining the legal right to use medical marijuana to treat a debilitating medical condition under Illinois' Medical Marijuana Law?

A patient or designated caregiver must first obtain a registry identification card from the IDPH by submitting a completed application [410 ILCS 130/55(a)]. A patient or designated caregiver can apply for a registry identification card in paper form or electronically [410 ILCS 130/60(a)(4)].

## 2-103. What does Illinois' Medical Marijuana Law application process involve or require?

The application includes, among other things: (1) receipt of a written certification from a physician that the use of medical marijuana is recommended for a diagnosed debilitating medical condition for the qualifying patient having a date no more than 90 days of the application date [410 ILCS 130/55(a)(1)]; (2) privacy waivers; (3) medical records support the existence and diagnoses of the medical condition [410 ILCS 130/55(a)(1)]; (4) payment of application or renewal fee [410 ILCS 130/55(a)(3)]; (5) the name of the registered dispensing organization that will be used by the patient [410 ILCS 130/55(a)(7)]; and (6) background checks for patients (and any designated caregiver of patient)[410 ILCS 130/55(a)(9)] which includes submitting a full set of fingerprints to the IDPH for the purpose of obtaining a state and federal criminal records check, unless the IDPH waives the submission of a qualifying patient's complete fingerprints based on (i) the severity of the patient's illness and (ii) the inability of the qualifying patient to obtain those fingerprints, provided that a complete criminal background check is conducted by the Department of State Police prior to the issuance of a registry identification card [410 ILCS 130/65(d)].

**2-104. How long does it take for the IDPH to approve or deny an application to be a registered medical marijuana patient (user) or registered designated caregiver – is there a time limit?**

The IDPH must either approve or deny a patient's or designated caregiver's application within thirty (30) days of receiving a completed new user application or renewal application [410 ILCS 130/60(a)(1)].

**2-105. Under what grounds can the IDPH deny a patient's application or renewal of a registry identification card to lawfully use medical marijuana?**

An application can be denied if an applicant patient: (1) did not provide the application requirements and information requests [410 ILCS 130/65(a)(1)]; (2) had his or her registry card revoked [410 ILCS 130/65(a)(2]; (3) did not meet the requirements of the Medical Marijuana Law [410 ILCS 130/65(a)(3)];  (4) provided false information to the IDPH [410 ILCS 130/65(a)(4)]; or (5) was convicted of a felony under the Illinois Controlled Substances Act, Cannabis Act, or Methamphetamine Control and Community Protection Act, or a similar provision in a local ordinance or other jurisdiction [410 ILCS 130/65(b)].

**2-106. Under what grounds can the IDPH deny a designated caregiver's application or renewal of a registry identification card to lawfully administer medical marijuana to a patient?**

An caregiver's application can be denied by the IDPH if [*see generally*, 410 ILCS 130/65(c)(1)]: (1) the caregiver is not 21 or older 410 ILCS 130/10(i)(1]; (2) the applicant caregiver was convicted of a felony under the Illinois Controlled Substances Act, Cannabis Act, or Methamphetamine Control and Community Protection Act, or a similar provision in a local ordinance or other jurisdiction [410 ILCS 130/10(i)(3) referencing 410 ILCS 130/65(b)]; (3) the applicant caregiver is seeking to serve as a caregiver to more than one patient using medical marijuana [410 ILCS 130/10(i)(4)]; (4) the applicant caregiver did not provide the application requirements and information requests [410 ILCS 130/65(c)(2)]; (5) the patient for whom the applicant caregiver wishes to administer medical marijuana does not qualify for a registry card [410 ILCS 130/65(c)(3)]; (6) the applicant caregiver had his or her registry card revoked [410 ILCS 130/65(c)[4]; or (7) the applicant caregiver provided false information to the IDPH [410 ILCS 130/65(c)(5)].

## 2-107. How long does it take to be issued a registry identification card to lawfully use medical marijuana in Illinois?

The IDPH must issue registry identification cards to a patient or designated caregiver within fifteen (15) business days of approving a new user application or renewal application [410 ILCS 130/60(a)(2)].

## 2-108. What if the IDPH fails to approve or deny a patient or designated caregiver application for a registry card?

If the IDPH fails to grant or deny a renewal application received within the required 30-day time period [410 ILCS 130/60(a)(1)], then the renewal application is deemed approved and the registered qualifying patient or registered designated caregiver may continue to use the expired identification card until the IDPH denies the renewal or issues a new identification card [410 ILCS 130/70(c)]. In a latter part of the Act, it further states that if the IDPH fails to issue a valid identification card in response to a valid application or renewal submitted under the Act or fails to issue a verbal or written notice of denial of the application within 30 days of its submission, the identification card is deemed granted, and a copy of the registry identification application, including a valid written certification in the case of patients, or renewal shall be deemed a valid registry identification card [410 ILCS 130/170(b)].

## 2-109. What if a patient's or designated caregiver's application for a registration card is denied – Are they out of luck?

Not necessarily. A denial of an application or renewal is considered a final Department action, subject to judicial review [410 ILCS 130/155 and 410 ILCS 130/185(b)]. Thus, if you wish to appeal the determination, jurisdiction and venue for judicial review are vested in the Illinois Circuit Courts [410 ILCS 130/65(f) and 410 ILCS 130/185(b)].

## 2-110. How long is a patient's or designated caregiver's registration ID card to use medical marijuana (or serve as a designated caregiver to a medical marijuana user) valid, and when do I need to renew my card?

A registration card is valid for one (1) year [410 ILCS 130/70(d)]. To maintain a valid registration identification card, a registered qualifying patient and caregiver must annually resubmit, at least forty-five (45) days prior to the expiration date stated on the registry identification card, a completed renewal application, renewal fee, and accompanying documentation as described in IDPH rules [410 ILCS 130/70(c)].

**2-111. Is the IDPH required to notify a patient or designated caregiver notice that his or her registration card will expire (and that they need to renew their registry card)?**

Yes. The IDPH must send a notification to a registered qualifying patient or registered designated caregiver 90 days before the expiration of the registered qualifying patient's or registered designated caregiver's identification card [410 ILCS 130/70(c)].

**2-112. What is the legal amount of medical marijuana that can be possessed by registered patients?**

The Act allows 2.5 ounces of usable Cannabis to be possessed at one time. This is referred to as an "*adequate supply*." [410 ILCS 130/10(a)(1); 410 ILCS 130/30(g)]

**2-113. Can a registered patient ever obtain permission to use or possess more than 2.5 ounces of medical marijuana?**

Yes. A patient may apply for a waiver from a physician to obtain more than 2.5 ounces of medical marijuana if there is a substantial medical basis necessitating more than the adequate supply of 2.5 ounce [410 ILCS 130/10(a)(2); 410 ILCS 130/30(g)].

**2-114. Is there a *special* tax that a registered patient or designated caregiver (under Illinois' Medical Marijuana Law) subject to pay?**

No, the Medical Cannabis Cultivation Privilege Tax ([410 ILCS 130/190)] is imposed only upon cultivation centers for the privilege of cultivating medical marijuana (at a rate of 7% of the sales price per ounce) [410 ILCS 130/200(a)]. This Medical Cannabis Cultivation Privilege Tax is not the responsibility of a qualifying patient 410 ILCS 130/200(a)]. However, medical marijuana patients will be subject to the 1% retail sales tax (as of 2014) that is imposed on the sale of over-the-counter and prescription medication in Illinois.

**2-115. What medical conditions may qualify a patient for medical marijuana use?**

Cancer, glaucoma, HIV, AIDS, hepatitis C, ALS (Lou Gehrig's Disease), Crohn's disease, agitation of Alzheimer's disease, cachexia/wasting syndrome, muscular dystrophy, severe fibromyalgia, spinal cord disease, including but not limited to arachnoiditis,

Tarlov cysts, hydromyelia, syringomyelia, spinal cord injury, traumatic brain injury and post-concussion syndrome, Multiple Sclerosis, Arnold-Chiari malformation & Syringomyelia, Spinocerebellar Ataxia (SCA), Parkinson's, Tourette's, Myoclonus, Dystonia, Reflex Sympathetic Dystrophy, RSD (Complex Regional Pain Syndromes Type I), Causalgia, CRPS (Complex Regional Pain Syndromes Type II), Neurofibromatosis, Chronic Inflammatory Demyelinating Polyneuropathy, Sjogren's syndrome, Lupus, Interstitial Cystitis, Myasthenia Gravis, Hydrocephalus, nail-patella syndrome, or the treatment of these conditions; or any other debilitating medical condition or its treatment shall be added by the Department of Public Health. [410 ILCS 130/5(h)(1) and (2)]

**2-116. As a patient seeking the lawful use of medical marijuana, what if my medical condition is not listed as a qualifying condition, but I believe medical marijuana could relieve my pain -- Am I out of luck?**

No. Any citizen may petition the IDPH to add a debilitating condition or treatment to the list of qualifying conditions. The petition must be approved or denied with 180 days. A denial is eligible for judicial review with the Illinois Circuit Courts [410 ILCS 130/155, 410 ILCS 130/45, and 410 ILCS 130/185(b)].

**2-117. Do registered medical marijuana users have the right to reimbursement for medical marijuana from a government medical assistance program or through health insurance?**

No. Neither government medical assistance programs nor through health insurance companies are required to reimburse or cover a patient's medical marijuana use [410 ILCS 130/40(d)].

**2-118. I am a registered medical marijuana patient and I want to change the person who is registered as my designated caregiver – what do I need to do?**

Before a registered qualifying patient changes his or her designated caregiver, the qualifying patient must notify the IDPH [410 ILCS 130/75(a)(3)]. Furthermore, if a registered qualifying patient ceases to be a registered qualifying patient or changes his or her registered designated caregiver, the IDPH must promptly notify the designated caregiver. The registered designated caregiver's protections afforded under the Medical Marijuana Law (as to that qualifying patient) will expire 15 days after notification by the Department [410 ILCS 130/75(c)]. A cardholder who fails to make a notification to the

IDPH is subject to a civil infraction, punishable by a penalty of no more than $150 [410 ILCS 130/75(d)].

**2-119. I am a registered medical marijuana patient and lost my registration card – what do I need to do to obtain a replacement registration identification card – what about my designated caregiver (if applicable)?**

If a registered cardholder loses his or her registry identification card, he or she shall must notify the IDPH within ten (10) days of becoming aware the card has been lost [410 ILCS 130/75(a)(4)]. When the IDPH is notified of a lost card, change of address, change of medical condition or designated caregiver, but remains eligible to use medical marijuana under Illinois' Medical Marijuana Law, the IDPH must issue the cardholder a new registry identification card with a new random alphanumeric identification number within 15 business days of receiving the updated information and a fee as specified in IDPH rules. If the person notifying the IDPH is a registered qualifying patient, the IDPH must also issue his or her registered designated caregiver, if any, a new registry identification card within 15 business days of receiving the updated information [410 ILCS 130/75(b)]. A cardholder who fails to make a notification to the IDPH is subject to a civil infraction, punishable by a penalty of no more than $150 [410 ILCS 130/75(d)].

**2-120. What other responsibilities or obligations do I need to comply with under Illinois' Marijuana Law as a registered medical marijuana *patient*?**

- *Notice of new address of patient*. A registered qualifying patient shall notify the IDPH of any change in his or her name or address within 10 days of the change [410 ILCS 130/75(a)(1)]. A cardholder who fails to make a notification to the IDPH is subject to a civil infraction, punishable by a penalty of no more than $150 [410 ILCS 130/75(d)].

- *Notice of change in patient's medical condition*. A registered qualifying patient shall notify the IDPH of any change in his or her medical condition (in the opinion of his or her treating physician) if he or she no longer suffers from the debilitating medical condition within 10 days of the change [410 ILCS 130/75(a)(1)]. A cardholder who fails to make a notification to the IDPH is subject to a civil infraction, punishable by a penalty of no more than $150 [410 ILCS 130/75(d)]. If the registered qualifying patient's certifying physician notifies the IDPH in writing that either the registered qualifying patient has stopped suffering from his or her debilitating medical condition or that the physician no longer believes the patient would receive therapeutic or palliative benefit from the medical use of cannabis, the card is deemed null and void. The registered qualifying patient shall have 15 days to destroy his or her remaining medical cannabis and related paraphernalia [410 ILCS 130/75(f)].

- *Change of patient's dispensing organization.* A registered qualifying patient shall notify the IDPH of any change to his or her designated registered dispensing organization [410 ILCS 130/75(e)].

## 2-121. What other responsibilities or obligations under Illinois' Marijuana Law does a *designated caregiver* for a medical marijuana patient need to comply?

- *Notice of new address of designated caregiver or death of the marijuana patient.* A registered designated caregiver shall notify the Department of Public Health of any change in his or her name or address, or if the designated caregiver becomes aware the registered qualifying patient passed away, within 10 days of the change. [410 ILCS 130/75(a)(2)]. A cardholder who fails to make a notification to the IDPH is subject to a civil infraction, punishable by a penalty of no more than $150 [410 ILCS 130/75(d)].

## EMPLOYER/EMPLOYEE LEGAL ISSUES

## 3-100. Can an Illinois employer adopt rules to regulate, restrict or prohibit its employees and/or visitors from the medical use of marijuana on the employer's property?

Yes, an Illinois employer has the authority to adopt reasonable regulations concerning the consumption, storage, and time keeping requirements for its employees [410 ILCS 130/50(a)], including restricting the use of medical marijuana altogether on its (whether owned or leased) property [410 ILCS 130/30(h)]. Unlike the requirement under Illinois' Concealed Firearm Act, an employer need not be the actual property owner of the underlying real property to restrict the use of medical marijuana at its work location.

## 3-101. Can an employer penalize or discipline an employee for holding the status as a medical marijuana user?

No. An employer is prohibited from penalizing an employee for holding the status as a medical marijuana user, *unless* failing to do so would place the employer in violation of federal law or put it in jeopardy of losing a monetary or licensing-related benefit under a federal law or rule. [410 ILCS 130/40(a)(1)]

## 3-102. Can an Illinois employer adopt or maintain and enforce a drug testing, zero-tolerance, or drug-free workplace?

Yes, so long as the policy is applied in a nondiscriminatory manner. [410 ILCS 130/50(b)]

## 3-103. Can an Illinois employer discipline a registered medical marijuana-using employee who violates a zero-tolerance or drug-free workplace policy?

Yes. An Illinois employer can discipline a registered medical marijuana user/employee for violating a zero-tolerance or drug-free workplace policy [410 ILCS 130/50(c)].

## 3-104. Can an Illinois employer discipline a registered medical marijuana-using employee who fails a employer drug test (due to the positive test of marijuana) -- Could I then be in violation of the federal Americans with Disabilities Act of 1990 (ADA)?

Yes an employer can discipline a registered medical marijuana-using employee who fails a employer drug test due to the positive test of marijuana, but only if failing to discipline the employee would put the employer in violation of federal law or cause it to lose a federal contract or funding [410 ILCS 130/50(d)]. Remember, Illinois' Compassionate Use of Medical Cannabis Pilot Program is solely an Illinois law recognized by the State of Illinois - The federal government does not have an equivalent federal medical marijuana statute to provide patients the lawfully use medical marijuana to treat a debilitating condition. Therefore, the rights and protections afforded under Illinois' law are not recognized by the federal government.

In May of 2012, the Ninth Circuit Court of Appeals held that the Americans with Disabilities Act (**ADA**) does not prohibit discrimination based on medical marijuana use even if it is done under a doctor's supervision in accordance with state law. The only way the ADA would apply is of such use is authorized under federal law. See, *James v. City of Costa Mesa*, 684 F.3d 825 (9th Cir. 2012).

## 3-105. Can the use of medical marijuana serve as a defense to a third party a failed employer drug test?

No. Nothing under Illinois' Medical Marijuana Law creates a defense to a failed drug test. [410 ILCS 130/50(e)].

### 3-106. From an employer's standpoint, when is an employee who uses medical marijuana considered "impaired"?

An employer may consider a registered qualifying patient/employee to be impaired when he or she manifests specific, articulable symptoms while working that decrease or lessen his or her performance of the duties or tasks of the employee's job position. For example, symptoms of the employee's speech, physical dexterity, agility, coordination, demeanor, irrational or unusual behavior, negligence or carelessness in operating equipment or machinery, disregard for the safety of the employee or others, or involvement in an accident that results in serious damage to equipment or property, disruption of a production or manufacturing process, or carelessness that results in any injury to the employee or others support the existence of an impairment. [410 ILCS 130/50(f)]

### 3-107. If an employer has grounds to believe and medical marijuana impairment exists and disciplines the employee, is the employer's decision to discipline deemed final and enforceable?

No. An employer must afford the employee a reasonable opportunity to contest the basis of the determination/disciplinary action. [410 ILCS 130/50(f)]

### 3-108. Does an employer face liability if, in error, it takes disciplinary or investigatory action against an employee whom it believes is impaired from, used, possessed medical marijuana?

No, provided that the employer possesses a good-faith belief that the employee is impaired from, used, or possessed medical marijuana, there is no cause of action against an employer. [410 ILCS 130/50(g)(1) and (2)]

### 3-109. Can an employer escape liability from a cause of action by a third party who sustains injury or loss as a result of an employee's medical marijuana use?

Yes, provided that the employer did not know or have reason to know that the employee was impaired from using medical marijuana, there is no cause of action against an employer. [410 ILCS 130/50(g)(3)]

### 3-110. Are there any jobs or occupations that are restricted from using medical marijuana?

Yes. An active duty law enforcement officer, correctional officer, correctional probation officer, or firefighter cannot use medical cannabis. Also, a school bus driver or CDL license holder is prohibited from using medical marijuana.

### 3-111. Do IDPH, IDA, IDFPR or any other State agency or local government employees have any obligation to report offenses under the Act?

Yes, authorized employees of State or local law enforcement agencies must immediately notify the IDPH when any person in possession of a registry identification card has been determined by a court of law to have willfully violated the provisions of the Act or has pled guilty to the offense [410 ILCS 130/170(c)].

### 3-112. Are there consequences if an employee of the IDPH, IDA, IDFPR or any other State agency or local government employee unlawfully discloses private patient, designated caregiver, cultivation center, or dispensing organization information under the Act?

It is a Class B misdemeanor with a $1,000 fine for any person, including an employee or official of the IDPH, IDA, IDFPR or another State agency or local government, to breach the confidentiality of information obtained under this Act [410 ILCS 130/145(c)].

## HEALTH LAW / PHYSICIAN/ HEALTHCARE PROVIDER ISSUES

### 4-100. I am a physician. What exposure to liability, if any, do I have under the Act?

A physician who provides a written certification indicating that a patient is likely to receive therapeutic or palliative benefit from the use of medical marijuana to treat a patient's debilitating medical condition will not be liable for any criminal, disciplinary or civil penalty unless: (1) the written certification is provided to a patient not under the care for a debilitating medical condition; or (2) negligence in evaluating a patient's medical condition or standard of care. [410 ILCS 130/25(e)]

### 4-101. What healthcare professionals are allowed to certify a debilitating medical condition for purposes of prescribing medical marijuana?

A physician can certify that a patient has a debilitating medical condition and prescribe the use of medical marijuana under the Act, provided that he or she: (1) is licensed under the Medical Practice Act of 1987 in all its branches and in good standing; (2) holds a controlled substance license under Article III of the Illinois Controlled Substances Act; and (3) complies with the generally accepted medical practices. [410 ILCS 130/35(a)(1)].

**4-102 As a physician, what are the rules, regulations, and restrictions I need to be aware of and comply in order to properly certify that a patient has a debilitating medical condition for purposes of prescribing medical marijuana?**

CERTIFICATION RESTRICTIONS:

A physician CANNOT: (1) perform an examination of a patient remotely, including telemedicine [410 ILCS 130/35(a)(3); (2) receive any form or remuneration or kickback, except for the fee associated with the examination, in exchange from any patient, caregiver, cultivation center, dispensing organization certifying a qualifying patient to use medical marijuana [410 ILCS 130/35(b)(1)]; (3) offer a discount or any other value for a patient to use a particular primary caregiver or dispensing organization [410 ILCS 130/35(b)(2)]; (4) perform examinations on patients at a dispensatory, distribution center, or the address of an employee, officer, or medical cannabis organization [410 ILCS 130/35(b)(3)]; (5) hold a direct or indirect economic interest in, serve on a board of, or advertise in a cultivation center or dispensing organization, or is in a fee sharing arrangement with a physician who recommends medical marijuana [410 ILCS 130/35(b)(4), (5) and (7)]; (6) refer patients to a cultivation center, dispensing organization, or registered caregiver [410 ILCS 130/35(b)(6)].

COMPLIANCE REGULATIONS:

A physician must maintain a recordkeeping system for all patients for whom the physician recommended the use of medical marijuana (subject to review by the DPH and IDFPR upon request) [410 ILCS 130/35(a)(4)].

**4-103. Can medical marijuana be used in health care facilities, or is this deemed a "public place" and not allowed under the Act?**

Registered patients are prohibited from *smoking* medical marijuana in health care facilities such as hospitals, nursing homes, hospice care centers, and long-term care facilities since smoking is prohibited in such facilities under the Smoke Free Illinois Act. It is unclear whether use of medical marijuana infused food products will be permitted in health care facilities. The IDPH may adopt additional rules or guidance with respect to such use of medical marijuana infused products in health care facilities. [410 ILCS 130/30(a)(2)(F) and 410 ILCS 130/30(a)(4)]

**4-104. Can a healthcare provider deny or disqualify a person needed medical care because his or her status as a registered medical marijuana user?**

A registered user cannot be denied or disqualified from needed medical care [410 ILCS 130/40(a)(2)].

## BUSINESS LAW / BUSINESS ENTREPRENUER ISSUES

<u>REGISTERED CULTIVATION CENTERS</u>

**5-101. What is a medical marijuana cultivation center?**

A "cultivation center" means a facility operated by an organization or business that is registered by the Illinois Department of Agriculture (**IDA**) to perform necessary activities to provide only registered medical cannabis dispensing organizations with usable medical marijuana [410 ILCS 130/10(e)].

**5-102. What is a medical marijuana cultivation center agent?**

A "cultivation center agent" means a principal officer, board member, employee, or agent of a registered cultivation center who is 21 years of age or older and has not been convicted of an excluded offense [410 ILCS 130/10(f)].

**5-103. Who is in charge of the oversight/regulation of medical marijuana cultivation centers?**

The IDA is responsible for enforcing the provisions of the Act relating to the registration and oversight of cultivation centers. This includes the authority to revoke or suspend registrations for violations of this Act [410 ILCS 130/15(b)]. The IDPH adopts rules for the manufacture of medical cannabis-infused products, enforces these provisions, and for that purpose it may at all times enter every building, room, basement, enclosure, or premises occupied or used or suspected of being occupied or used for the production, preparation, manufacture for sale, storage, sale, distribution or transportation of medical cannabis edible products, to inspect the premises and all utensils, fixtures, furniture, and machinery used for the preparation of these products [410 ILCS 130/80(b)].

Also, local government also may enact reasonable zoning ordinances or resolutions, not in conflict with the Law or with IDA or IDPH rules, regulating registered medical cannabis cultivation centers; provided, however, that no local government (including a home rule unit) or school district may regulate registered medical cannabis organizations other than as provided in Law and may not unreasonably prohibit the cultivation, dispensing, and use of medical cannabis authorized by the Law [410 ILCS 130/140]. (NOTE: that this a denial and limitation under subsection (i) of Section 6 of Article VII of the Illinois Constitution on the concurrent exercise by home rule units of powers and functions exercised by the State).

APPLICATION FOR REGISTRATION CERTIFICATION

**5-104. I would like to apply for ownership and operation of a registered cultivation center in Illinois – what do I need to know and do?**

Below are just a few main prerequisites needed to be eligible to receive registration certification as a medical marijuana *cultivation center* in Illinois:

- AGE: You must be at least 21 years of age of to own, or serve as principal officer or board member of the cultivation center [410 ILCS 130/85(d)(3)].

- CRIMINAL CONVICTION/REVOCATION: No owner, officer, or board member seeking a registration to own and operate a cultivation center can have been convicted of an excluded offense (e.g., a violent crime, violation of controlled substance law that is a felony – unless waived by the reviewing Department for certain limited offenses [410 ILCS 130/10(I)]) [410 ILCS 130/85(e)(3)], had a registration revoked [410 ILCS 130/85(e)(4)], or been convicted of a felony under any federal or state law, among other possible exclusions [410 ILCS 130/85(e)(6)].

- LICENSING: A cultivation center may only operate if it has been issued a valid registration from the IDA after going through the application process [410 ILCS 130/85(d)].

- LIMITED CULTIVATION REGISTERATIONS GRANTED. The IDA may register up to 22 cultivation center registrations for operation under Illinois' Medical Marijuana Law. The IDA may not issue more than one registration per each Illinois State Police District boundary as specified on the date of January 1, 2013. However, the IDA may not issue less than the 22 registrations if there are qualified applicants who have applied with the Department [410 ILCS 130/85(a)].

- REGISTRATION: The registrations for cultivation centers must be issued and renewed annually as determined by administrative rule [410 ILCS 130/85(b) and 410 ILCS 130/90(a)].

**5-105. What does the application process entail to apply for a registration certification to operate a legal cultivation center for medical marijuana?**

When applying for a cultivation center registration certification, an applicant must submit the following in accordance with the IDA rules: (1) the proposed legal name of the cultivation center; (2) the proposed physical address of the cultivation center and description of the enclosed, locked facility as it applies to cultivation centers where medical cannabis will be grown, harvested, manufactured, packaged, or otherwise prepared for distribution to a dispensing organization; (3) the name, address, and date of birth of each principal officer and board member of the cultivation center, provided that all those individuals shall be at least 21 years of age; (4) any instance in which a business that any of the prospective board members of the cultivation center had managed or served on the board of the business and was convicted, fined, censured, or had a registration or license suspended or revoked in any administrative or judicial proceeding; (5) cultivation, inventory, and packaging plans; (6) proposed operating by-laws that include procedures for the oversight of the cultivation center, development and implementation of a plant monitoring system, medical cannabis container tracking system, accurate record keeping, staffing plan, and security plan reviewed by the Illinois State Police that are in accordance with IDA rules pursuant to the Medical Marijuana Law. A physical inventory must be performed of all plants and medical cannabis containers on a weekly basis; (7) experience with agricultural cultivation techniques and industry standards; (8) any academic degrees, certifications, or relevant experience with related businesses; (9) the identity of every person, association, trust, or corporation having any direct or indirect pecuniary interest in the cultivation center operation with respect to which the registration is sought. If the disclosed entity is a trust, the application shall disclose the names and addresses of the beneficiaries; if a corporation, the names and addresses of all stockholders and directors; if a partnership, the names and addresses of all partners, both general and limited; (10) verification from the Illinois State Police that all federal and state level background checks (with fingerprinting ) of the principal officer, board members, and registered agents have been conducted [410 ILCS 130/95(a) and (b)], and those individuals have not been convicted of an "excluded offense" (e.g., a violent crime, violation of controlled substance law that is a felony – unless waived by the reviewing Department for certain limited offenses [410 ILCS 130/10(l)]) [410 ILCS 130/85(e)(3)]; (11) provide a copy of the current local zoning ordinance to the IDA and verify that proposed cultivation center is in compliance with the local zoning rules (issued in accordance with Section 140); (12) an application fee set by the IDA; and (13) any other information required by the IDA, including, but not limited to a cultivation center applicant's experience with the cultivation of agricultural or horticultural products, operating an agriculturally related business, or operating a horticultural business [410 ILCS 130/85(d)(1)-(13)].

**5-106. What is the expected timeframe for the application process to be complete from the time of submission to receiving a decision from the IDA?**

The IDA must send applicants confirmation of receipt of the application [410 ILCS 130/100(a)(4)], and either approve or deny an application or renewal within thirty (30) days of receiving a completed application or renewal application and all supporting documentation [410 ILCS 130/100(a)(1)]. The IDA must also issue a cultivation center agent identification card to a qualifying agent within fifteen (15) business days of approving the application or renewal [410 ILCS 130/100(a)(2)].

**5-107. Are there conditions that could require the IDA to deny my application to obtain a registration to operate a legal cultivation center for medical marijuana?**

Yes, an application for a cultivation center permit *must* be denied by the IDA if any of the following conditions exist: (1) the applicant failed to submit the application materials required [410 ILCS 130/85(d)(1)-(13)], including if the applicant's plans do not satisfy the security, oversight, inventory, or recordkeeping rules issued by the IDA; (2) the applicant would violate local zoning rules (issued in accordance with Section 140); (3) one or more of the prospective principal officers or board members has been convicted of an "excluded offense" [410 ILCS 130/85(e)(3) and 410 ILCS 130/100(f)] (e.g., a violent crime, violation of a controlled substance law that is categorized as a felony – unless such felony is related to certain offenses related to reasonable amounts if medical marijuana and is waived by the reviewing Department [410 ILCS 130/10(l)]); (4) one or more of the prospective principal officers or board members has served as a principal officer or board member for a registered dispensing organization or cultivation center that has had its registration revoked; (5) one or more of the principal officers or board members is under 21 years of age; (6) a principal officer or board member of the cultivation center has been convicted of a felony under any federal or state law; (7) a principal officer or board member of the cultivation center has been convicted of any violation of Article 28 of the Criminal Code of 2012 (criminal offenses related to illegal gambling in Illinois), or substantially similar laws of any other jurisdiction; or (8) the person has submitted an application for a certificate under the Medical Marijuana Law which contains false information [410 ILCS 130/85(e)(1)-(8)].

**5-108. How often does a registration certification for a cultivation center need to be renewed – what is the process or procedure?**

Registrations must be renewed annually. A registered cultivation center must receive written notice 90 days from the IDA prior to the expiration of its current registration that the registration will expire. The IDA is required to grant a renewal application within 45 days of its receipt of the renewal application if the following conditions are satisfied: (1) the registered cultivation center submits a renewal application and the required renewal fee established; and (2) the IDA has not suspended the registration of the cultivation center or suspended or revoked the registration for violation of Illinois' Medical Marijuana Law or rules adopted therein [410 ILCS 130/90].

**5-109. What obligations must comply after I am approved for a cultivation center agent registration card?**

A cultivation center agent must keep his or her cultivation center agent identification card visible at all times when on the property of a cultivation center and during the transportation of medical cannabis to a registered dispensary organization [410 ILCS 130/100(b)]. Upon termination of employment of a cultivation center agent, his or her identification cards must be immediately returned to the cultivation center [410 ILCS 130/100(c)]. Any card lost by a cultivation center agent must be reported to the Illinois State Police and the IDA immediately upon discovery of the loss [410 ILCS 130/100(e)].

**5-110. CULTIVATION CENTER FACILITY COMPLIANCE**

Owners and operators of medical marijuana cultivation centers must make certain they comply with the rules and regulations concerning the cultivation center facility upon approval of an approved application to lawfully own and operate a medical marijuana cultivation center in Illinois. Some of the regulations include:

- INVENTORY: The operating documents of a registered cultivation center shall include procedures for the oversight of the cultivation center, a marijuana plant monitoring system including a physical inventory recorded weekly, a marijuana container system including a physical inventory recorded weekly, accurate record keeping, and a staffing plan [410 ILCS 130/105(a)].

- SECURITY SYSTEM: A registered cultivation center shall implement a security plan reviewed by the State Police and including but not limited to: facility access controls, perimeter intrusion detection systems, personnel identification systems, 24-hour surveillance system to monitor the interior and exterior of the registered cultivation center facility and accessible to authorized law enforcement and the IDFPR in real-time [410 ILCS 130/105(b)].

- LOCATION: A registered cultivation center may not be located within 2,500 feet of the property line of a pre-existing public or private preschool or elementary or secondary school or day care center, day care home, group day care home, part day child care facility, or an area zoned for residential use [410 ILCS 130/105(c)].

- CONTROLLED ENVIRONMENT: All cultivation of cannabis for distribution to a registered dispensing organization must take place in an enclosed, locked facility as it applies to cultivation centers at the physical address provided to the IDA during the registration process. The cultivation center location must only be accessed by the cultivation center agents working for the registered cultivation center, IDA staff performing inspections, IDPH staff performing inspections, law enforcement or other emergency personnel, and contractors working on jobs unrelated to medical cannabis, such as installing or maintaining security devices or performing electrical wiring [410 ILCS 130/105(d)].

- SALE AND DISTRIBUTION: A cultivation center may not sell or distribute any cannabis to any individual or entity other than a dispensary organization registered under Illinois' Medical Marijuana Law [410 ILCS 130/105(e)].

- PACKAGING/LABELING: All harvested marijuana intended for distribution to a dispensing organization must be packaged in a labeled medical cannabis container and entered into a data collection system[410 ILCS 130/105(f)].

- DISQUALIFIED PERSONS: No person who has been convicted of an "excluded offense" (e.g., a violent crime, violation of controlled substance law that is a felony –

unless waived by the reviewing Department for certain limited offenses [410 ILCS 130/10(l)]) [410 ILCS 130/85(e)(3)], may be a cultivation center agent [410 ILCS 130/105(g)].

- LOSS OR THEFT: A cultivation center agent must notify local law enforcement, the Illinois State Police, and the IDA within 24 hours of the discovery of any loss or theft. Notification shall be made by phone or in-person, or by written or electronic communication [410 ILCS 130/105(j)].

- PESTICIDES: A cultivation center must comply with all State and federal rules and regulations regarding the use of pesticides [410 ILCS 130/105(k)].

- DISPOSAL: A cultivation center shall prior to the destruction, notify the Department of Agriculture and the State Police. All cannabis byproduct, scrap, and harvested cannabis not intended for distribution to a medical cannabis organization must be destroyed and disposed of pursuant to State law. The cultivation center shall keep record of the date of destruction and how much was destroyed. Documentation of destruction and disposal shall be retained at the cultivation center for a period of not less than 5 years [410 ILCS 130/180(a) – (d)].

## 5-111. Is an Illinois medical marijuana cultivation center subject to inspection?

Yes, the Act states that registered cultivation centers are subject to "random" inspection by the Illinois State Police [410 ILCS 130/105(h)], and the IDA [410 ILCS 130/105(i)]. However, another section of the Act indicates there must be "probable cause" to believe that the criminal laws of Illinois have been violated to warrant an inspection. Nevertheless, the search is conducted in conformity with the Illinois Constitution [410 ILCS 130/25(n)]. Furthermore, the IDPH may at all times enter every building, room, basement, enclosure, or premises occupied or used or suspected of being occupied or used for the production, preparation, manufacture for sale, storage, sale, distribution or transportation of medical cannabis edible products, to inspect the premises and all utensils, fixtures, furniture, and machinery used for the preparation of these products [410 ILCS 130/80(b)].

## 5-112. What tax is an Illinois medical marijuana cultivation center subject to pay, if any?

The Medical Cannabis Cultivation Privilege Tax ("**Privilege Tax**") ([410 ILCS 130/190)] is imposed upon the privilege of cultivating medical marijuana at a rate of 7% of the sales price per ounce [410 ILCS 130/200(a)]. This tax must be paid by a cultivation center and is not the responsibility of a dispensing organization [410 ILCS 130/200(a)]. This tax is in addition to all other occupation or privilege taxes imposed by the State of Illinois or by any municipal corporation or political subdivision thereof [410 ILCS 130/200(b)].

Every person/cultivation center subject to the Privilege Tax under the Law is required to apply to the Illinois Department of Revenue (**IDOR**) (upon a form prescribed and furnished by the Department) for a Certificate of Registration [410 ILCS 130/205(a)]. The Certificate of Registration permits the taxpayer to engage in a business which is taxable under this Act without registering separately with the IDOR [410 ILCS 130/205(a)].

It is worth noting that marijuana patients will be subject to the 1% retail sales tax (as of 2014) that is imposed on the sale over-the-counter and prescription medication in Illinois.

## 5-113. Are there tax filing obligations a cultivation center is required to comply with?

Yes, on or before the 20$^{th}$ day of each calendar month, every person subject to the Privilege Tax during the preceding calendar month shall file a return with the IDOR, stating: (1) The name of taxpayer; (2) The number of ounces of medical cannabis sold to a dispensary organization or a registered qualifying patient during the preceding calendar month; (3) The amount of tax due; (4) The signature of the taxpayer; and (5) Such other reasonable information as the IDOR may require [410 ILCS 130/210(1) – (5)].

## 5-114. What are the consequences of not complying with tax return filing obligations by a cultivation center?

If a cultivation center (taxpayer) fails to sign a return within thirty (30) days after the proper notice and demand for signature by the IDOR, the return shall be considered valid and any amount shown to be due on the return shall be deemed assessed. The taxpayer is then required to remit the amount of the tax due to the IDOR at the time the taxpayer files his or her return [410 ILCS 130/210(5)].

MEDICAL MARIJUANA PRODUCTS

## 5-115. Who is in charge of the oversight for marijuana-infused food products for consumption?

The IDPH is responsible for establishing, maintaining, and enforcing rules and a registry for marijuana-infused food products for consumption [410 ILCS 130/15(a)(4) and 410 ILCS 130/80(b)]. For such purposes, the IDPH may at all times enter every building, room, basement, enclosure, or premises occupied or used or suspected of being occupied or used for the production, preparation, manufacture for sale, storage, sale, distribution or transportation of medical cannabis edible products, to inspect the premises and all utensils, fixtures, furniture, and machinery used for the preparation of these products [410 ILCS 130/80(b)].

## 5-116. Can marijuana cultivation centers make marijuana food products that require refrigeration or cooking?

No cannabis infused products that requires refrigeration or hot-holding shall be manufactured at a cultivation center for sale or distribution at a dispensing organization due to the potential for food-borne illness [410 ILCS 130/80(a)(1)].

## 5-117. With respect to the manufacture of medical marijuana and medically-infused marijuana food products, as a cultivation center, what product regulations must I comply?

- PACKAGING: All medical marijuana and medically-infused marijuana food products shall be individually wrapped at the original point of preparation [410 ILCS 130/80(a)(3)]. Cannabis infused products for sale or distribution at a dispensing organization must be prepared by an approved staff member of a registered cultivation center [410 ILCS 130/80(a)(5)]. The packaging of the medical cannabis infused product must conform to the labeling requirements of the Illinois Food, Drug and Cosmetic Act and must include the following information on each product offered for sale or distribution: (A) the name and address of the registered cultivation center where the item was manufactured; (B) the common or usual name of the item; (C) all ingredients of the item, including any colors, artificial flavors, and preservatives, listed in descending order by predominance of weight shown with common or usual names; (D) the following phrase: "*This product was produced in a medical cannabis cultivation center not subject to public health inspection that may also process common food allergens.*"; (E) allergen labeling as specified in the Federal

Food, Drug and Cosmetics Act, Federal Fair Packaging and Labeling Act, and the Illinois Food, Drug and Cosmetic Act; (F) the pre-mixed total weight (in ounces or grams) of usable cannabis in the package; (G) a warning that the item is a medical cannabis infused product and not a food must be distinctly and clearly legible on the front of the package; (H) a clearly legible warning emphasizing that the product contains medical cannabis and is intended for consumption by registered qualifying patients only; and (I) date of manufacture and "use by date" [410 ILCS 130/80(a)(3)(A) through (I)].

- SUPERVISION. A cultivation center that prepares cannabis infused products for sale or distribution at a dispensing organization shall be under the operational supervision of a Department of Public Health certified food service sanitation manager [410 ILCS 130/80(a)(6)].

VIOLATIONS BY CULTIVATION CENTER

**5-118. My cultivation center has been accused of creating public health hazards – what can I expect?**

If a local health organization has a reasonable belief that a cultivation center's cannabis-infused product poses a public health hazard, it may refer the cultivation center to the IDPH. If the IDPH finds that a cannabis-infused product poses a health hazard, it may without administrative procedure to bond, bring an action for immediate injunctive relief to require that action be taken as the court may deem necessary to meet the hazard of the cultivation center [410 ILCS 130/80(c)].

**5-119. My cultivation center was found in violation under the Act – What consequences may I be facing?**

Notwithstanding any possible criminal penalties, the IDA may suspend or revoke a cultivation center's registration granted under Illinois' Medical Marijuana Law for violations [410 ILCS 130/110(a) and 410 ILCS 130/185(a)]. All administrative hearings under the Act are conducted in accordance with the IDPH's rules governing administrative hearings [410 ILCS 130/175]. A suspension or revocation is seemed a final agency action subject to judicial review by the Illinois Circuit Court [410 ILCS 130/155, 410 ILCS 130/110(b), and 410 ILCS 130/185(b)].

REGISTERED DISPENSATORY ORGANIZATIONS

## 5-120. What is a medical marijuana dispensing organization?

A "medical cannabis dispensing organization," or "dispensing organization," or "dispensary organization" means a facility operated by an organization or business that is registered by the IDFPR to acquire medical cannabis from a registered cultivation center for the purpose of dispensing marijuana, paraphernalia, or related supplies and educational materials to registered qualifying patients [410 ILCS 130/10(o)].

## 5-121. Who is considered a medical marijuana dispensing organization agent?

A "medical cannabis dispensing organization agent" or "dispensing organization agent" means a principal officer, board member, employee, or agent of a registered medical marijuana dispensing organization who is 21 years of age or older and has not been convicted of an excluded offense [410 ILCS 130/10(p)].

## 5-122. Who is in charge of the oversight/regulation of medical marijuana dispensing organizations?

The Illinois Department of Financial and Professional Regulation (**IDFPR**) is responsible for enforcing the provisions of the Law relating to the registration and oversight of the dispensing organizations. This includes the authority to revoke or suspend registrations for violations of this Law [410 ILCS 130/15(c)]. Also, local government also may enact reasonable zoning ordinances or resolutions, not in conflict with the Law or with IDA or IDPH rules, regulating registered medical cannabis dispensing organizations; provided, however, that no local government (including a home rule unit) or school district may regulate registered medical cannabis organizations other than as provided in Law and may not unreasonably prohibit the cultivation, dispensing, and use of medical cannabis authorized by the Law [410 ILCS 130/140]. (NOTE: that this a denial and limitation under subsection (i) of Section 6 of Article VII of the Illinois Constitution on the concurrent exercise by home rule units of powers and functions exercised by the State).

APPLICATION FOR REGISTRATION

## 5-123. I would like to apply for ownership and operation of a registered dispensatory organization in Illinois – what do I need to know and do?

Below are just a few main prerequisites/information needed to be eligible to apply to receive registration as a medical marijuana *dispensatory organization* in Illinois:

- LIMITED NUMBER OF REGISTRATIONS. The IDFPR may issue up to 60 dispensing organization registrations for operation. The IDHPR may not issue less than the 60 registrations if there are qualified applicants who have applied with the IDFPR. The organizations shall be geographically dispersed throughout Illinois to allow all registered qualifying patients reasonable proximity and access to a dispensing organization [410 ILCS 130/115(a)].

- LICENSE: A dispensing organization may only operate if it has been issued a registration from the IDFPR [410 ILCS 130/115(b)].

- AGE: Every owner, officer, board member must be at least 21-years-old [410 ILCS 130/115(c)(4)].

- NON-PATIENT/CAREGIVER: None of the principal officers or board members can be a registered qualified patient or a registered caregiver [410 ILCS 130/115(f)(7)].

**5-124. What does the application process entail to apply for a registration to operate a legal dispensing organization for medical marijuana?**

When applying for a dispensing organization registration, an applicant must submit the following in accordance with the IDFPR rules: (1) a non-refundable application fee to the IDFPR [410 ILCS 130/115(c)(1) and (e)] ; (2) the proposed legal name of the dispensing organization [410 ILCS 130/115(c)(2)]; (3) the proposed physical address of the dispensing organization [410 ILCS 130/115(c)(3)]; (4) the name, address, and date of birth of each principal officer and board member of the dispensing organization, provided that all those individuals shall be at least 21 years of age [410 ILCS 130/115(c)(4)]; (5) information, in writing, regarding any instances in which a business or not-for-profit that any of the prospective board members managed or served on the board was convicted, fined, censured, or had a registration suspended or revoked in any administrative or judicial proceeding [410 ILCS 130/115(c)(5)]; (6) proposed operating by-laws that include procedures for the oversight of the medical cannabis dispensing organization and procedures to ensure accurate record keeping and security measures that are in accordance with the rules applied by the IDFPR under the Law. The by-laws must include a description of the enclosed, locked facility where medical cannabis will be stored by the dispensing organization [410 ILCS 130/115(c)(6)]; and (7) signed statements from each dispensing organization agent stating that they will not divert medical cannabis [410 ILCS 130/115(c)(7)].

An applicant (prospective dispensing organization agents) must also submit to a background check, which includes fingerprinting to the IDFPR for the purpose of obtaining a state and federal criminal records check [410 ILCS 130/115(d)]. The IDFPR has the right to exchange this data with the Illinois State Police and the FBI without disclosing that the records check is related to this the application under the Law [410 ILCS 130/115(c)(7)].

**5-125. What is the expected timeframe for the application process to be complete from the time of submission to receiving a decision from the IDFPR?**

The IDFPR must approve or deny an application or renewal within thirty (30) days of receiving a completed application or renewal application and all supporting documentation [410 ILCS 130/120(a)(1)], and issue a dispensing organization agent identification card to a qualifying agent within fifteen (15) business days of approving the application or renewal [410 ILCS 130/120(a)(1)].

**5-126. Are there conditions that could require the IDFPR to deny my application to obtain a registration to operate a legal dispensing organization for medical marijuana?**

Yes, an application for a dispensing organization permit *must* be denied by the IDFPR if any of the following conditions exist: (1) the applicant fails to submit all of the application materials required, including if the applicant's plans do not satisfy the security, oversight, or recordkeeping rules issued by the IDFPR; (2) the applicant would not be in compliance with local zoning rules in the Law[410 ILCS 130/140]; (3) the applicant does not meet the requirements of Section 130 of the Law (compliance regulations for operating a dispensing organization facility); (4) one or more of the prospective principal officers or board members has been convicted of an "excluded offense" [410 ILCS 130/120(e)] (e.g., an "excluded offense" is a violent crime, violation of controlled substance law that is a felony – unless waived by the reviewing Department for certain limited offenses [410 ILCS 130/10(l)]) [410 ILCS 130/85(e)(3)]; (5) one or more of the prospective principal officers or board members has served as a principal officer or board member for a registered medical marijuana dispensing organization that has had its registration revoked; (6) one or more of the principal officers or board members is under 21 years of age; and (7) one or more of the principal officers or board members is a registered qualified patient or a registered caregiver [410 ILCS 130/115(f)(1) – (7)].

**5-127. What obligations must I comply after I am approved for a dispensing organization registration card?**

A dispensing agent must keep his or her identification card visible at all times when on the property of a dispensing organization [410 ILCS 130/120(b)]. The dispensing organization agent identification cards must be immediately returned to the dispensing organization upon termination of employment [410 ILCS 130/120(d) – note: this section of the Law actually states that the registration ID card must be returned to the *cultivation center*, but the author believes this a legislative drafting error]. Any card lost by a dispensing organization agent shall be reported to the Illinois State Police and the Department of Agriculture immediately upon discovery of the loss [410 ILCS 130/120(e)].

**5-128. How often does a registration for a dispensing organization need to be renewed – what is the process or procedure?**

The registered dispensing organization must renew its certificate of registration on an annual basis. The registered dispensing organization must receive written notice from the IDFPR ninety (90) days prior to the expiration of its current registration advising it that the registration will expire. The IDFPR must grant a renewal application within forty-five (45) days of its submission if the following conditions are satisfied: (1) the registered dispensing organization submits a renewal application and the required renewal fee; and (2) the IDFPR has not suspended the registered dispensing organization or suspended or revoked the registration for violation of the Law [410 ILCS 130/125(e)(1) and (2)].

**5-129. What if I failed to renew my certificate of registration with the IDFPR for my dispensing organization?**

If a dispensing organization fails to renew its registration prior to expiration, the dispensing organization must stop its operations until registration is renewed [410 ILCS 130/125(b)]. Similarly, if a dispensing organization agent fails to renew his or her registration prior to its expiration, he or she must stop to working or volunteering at a dispensing organization until his or her registration is renewed [410 ILCS 130/125(c)]. Any dispensing organization that continues to operate or dispensing agent that continues to work or volunteer at a dispensing organization that fails to renew its registration shall be subject to penalty provided in Section 130 of the Law [410 ILCS 130/125(d) and 410 ILCS 130/130(n)].

**5-130. DISPENSING ORGANIZATION FACILITY COMPLIANCE**

Owners and operators of medical marijuana dispensing organization facilities must comply with the rules and regulations concerning its dispensing organization facility upon approval of an approved application to lawfully own and operate a medical marijuana dispensing organization in Illinois. Some of the rules and regulations include: (i) A dispensing organization must maintain operating documents which shall include procedures for the oversight of the registered dispensing organization and procedures to ensure accurate recordkeeping [410 ILCS 130/130(b)]; (ii) A dispensing organization must implement appropriate security measures, as provided by rule, to deter and prevent the theft of marijuana and unauthorized entrance into areas containing marijuana [410 ILCS 130/130(c)]; (iii) A dispensing organization may not be located within 1,000 feet of the property line of a pre-existing public or private preschool or elementary or secondary school or day care center, day care home, group day care home, or part day child care facility [410 ILCS 130/130(d)]; (iv) A registered dispensing organization may not be located in a house, apartment, condominium, or an area zoned for residential use [410 ILCS 130/130(d) and 410 ILCS 130/140]; (v) A dispensing organization is prohibited from acquiring marijuana from anyone other than a registered cultivation center [410 ILCS 130/130(e)]; (vi) A dispensing organization is prohibited from obtaining marijuana from outside the State of Illinois [410 ILCS 130/130(e)]; (vii) A registered dispensing organization is prohibited from dispensing marijuana for any purpose except to assist registered qualifying patients with the medical use of marijuana directly or through the qualifying patients' designated caregivers [410 ILCS 130/130(f)]; (viii) The area in a dispensing organization where medical marijuana is stored can only be accessed by dispensing organization agents working for the dispensing organization, IDFPR staff performing inspections, law enforcement or other emergency personnel, and contractors working on jobs unrelated to medical cannabis, such as installing or maintaining security devices or performing electrical wiring [410 ILCS 130/130(g)]; (ix) A dispensing organization may not permit any person to consume cannabis on the property of a medical cannabis organization [410 ILCS 130/130(l)]; and (x) A dispensing organization may not share office space with a physician [410 ILCS 130/130(m)].

**5-131. Is an Illinois medical marijuana dispensing organization subject to inspection?**

Yes, dispensing organizations are subject to "random" inspection and cannabis testing by the IDFPR and Illinois State Police [410 ILCS 130/130(o)]. However, another section of the Act indicates there must be "probable cause" to believe that the criminal laws of Illinois have been violated and the search is conducted in conformity with the Illinois Constitution [410 ILCS 130/25(n)]. Furthermore, the IDPH may at all times enter every building, room, basement, enclosure, or premises occupied or used or suspected of being occupied or used for the production, preparation, manufacture for sale, storage, sale, distribution or transportation of medical cannabis edible products, to inspect the premises and all utensils, fixtures, furniture, and machinery used for the preparation of these products [410 ILCS 130/80(b)].

DISPENSING ORGANIZATION RETAIL SALES COMPLIANCE

**5-132. Who is in charge of the oversight for marijuana-infused food products for consumption?**

The Illinois Department of Public Health (**IDPH**) is responsible for establishing, maintaining, and enforcing rules and a registry for marijuana-infused food products for consumption [410 ILCS 130/15(a)(4) and 410 ILCS 130/80(b)].

**5-133. What retail sales rules and regulations does a dispensing organization need to comply?**

Dispensing organization effectively serve as the retail storefronts for patients in need of medical marijuana. As such, every registered dispensing organization must understand and comply with certain medical marijuana sales regulations required under the Law.

- *Store Signage.* Any dispensing organization that sells edible cannabis infused products must display a sign (no smaller than 24" tall by 36" wide, with typed letters no smaller than 2") that states the following: *"Edible cannabis infused products were produced in a kitchen not subject to public health inspections that may also process common food allergens."* The sign shall be clearly visible and readable by customers and shall be written in English [410 ILCS 130/80(a)(4)].

- *Limit on Sales Quantity of Medical Marijuana.* A dispensing organization may not dispense more than 2.5 ounces of medical marijuana to a registered qualifying patient, directly or via a designated caregiver in any 14-day period [410 ILCS 130/130(h) and [410 ILCS 130/25(l)], unless the qualifying patient has a valid

IDPH-approved quantity waiver [410 ILCS 130/30(g)]. Medical cannabis may not be dispensed more frequently or in larger amounts than as permitted under the Law [410 ILCS 130/135(3)].

- *Verification of Valid Registration ID:* Before medical marijuana may be dispensed to a designated caregiver or a registered qualifying patient, a dispensing organization agent must determine that the individual is a current cardholder in the verification system and must verify each of the following: (1) that the registry identification card presented to the registered dispensing organization is valid; (2) that the person presenting the card is the person identified on the registry identification card presented to the dispensing organization agent; (3) that the dispensing organization is the designated dispensing organization for the registered qualifying patient who is obtaining the cannabis directly or via his or her designated caregiver; and (4) that the registered qualifying patient has not exceeded his or her adequate supply [410 ILCS 130/130(i)(1) – (4)].

- *Recordkeeping Requirement.* Dispensing organizations must ensure compliance with the quantity limitation by maintaining internal, confidential records that include records specifying how much medical marijuana is dispensed to the registered qualifying patient and whether it was dispensed directly to the registered qualifying patient or to the designated caregiver. Each entry must include the date and time the cannabis was dispensed. Additional recordkeeping requirements may be set by rule [410 ILCS 130/130(j)].

- *Confidentiality of Patient Information.* The physician-patient privilege (as set forth by Section 8-802 of the Code of Civil Procedure) applies between a qualifying patient and a registered dispensing organization and its agents with respect to communications and records concerning qualifying patients' debilitating conditions [410 ILCS 130/130(k)].

- *Physician Referrals Prohibited.* A dispensing organization may not refer patients to a physician [410 ILCS 130/130(m)].

- *Disposal.* A dispensary organization shall prior to the destruction, notify the IDFRP and the Illinois State Police [410 ILCS 130/180(e)].

**5-134. When can a (newly designated) registered dispensing organization fill or refill a valid written certification for medical marijuana that is on file with the IDP where the designation has been transferred or changed by a patient or designated caregiver?**

Prior to dispensing medical marijuana (i.e., serving as the new replacement dispensing organization) under any written certification and the requirements of the Law, the new dispensing organization agent must: (i) advise the patient that the designated dispensing organization on file with the IDPH must be changed before he or she will be able to dispense any quantity of medical cannabis; (ii) determine that the patient is registered and in compliance with the IDPH under the requirements of the Law; (iii) notify the dispensing organization designated by the registered qualifying patient that the registered qualifying patient is changing his or her designation and the patient may no longer purchase medical marijuana at the original dispensing organization; and (iv) notify the IDPH of a patient's change in designation and receive confirmation from the IDPH that it has updated the registered qualifying patient database[410 ILCS 135/135(1)(A) – (D)].

**5-135. What marijuana food products are legal to sell at a registered dispensatory?**

Baked products infused with medical cannabis (such as brownies, bars, cookies, cakes), tinctures, and other non-refrigerated items are acceptable for sale at dispensing organizations [410 ILCS 130/80(a)(2)].

**5-136. I own a supermarket, convenient store, or other retail store – Can I sell marijuana food products under Illinois' Medical Marijuana Law?**

Baked products infused with medical cannabis (such as brownies, bars, cookies, cakes) are allowable for sale only at registered dispensing organizations [410 ILCS 130/80(a)(2)].

**5-137. Is there a special tax that an Illinois medical marijuana dispensing organization subject to pay?**

No, the only *special* tax set forth under the Law is the Medical Cannabis Cultivation Privilege Tax ([410 ILCS 130/190)], which is imposed only upon cultivation centers for the privilege of cultivating medical cannabis (at a rate of 7% of the sales price per ounce) [410 ILCS 130/200(a)]. This Medical Cannabis Cultivation Privilege Tax is not the responsibility of a dispensing organization or a qualifying patient 410 ILCS 130/200(a)].

However, dispensing organizations and registered patients will be subject to the applicable retail sales tax for over-the-counter and prescription medication (i.e., 1% as of 2014).

VIOLATIONS BY DISPENSING ORGANIZATION

**5-138. My dispensing organization was found in violation under the Act – What consequences may I be facing?**

Notwithstanding any other criminal penalties related to the unlawful possession of cannabis, the IDFPR may revoke, suspend, place on probation, reprimand, refuse to issue or renew, or take any other disciplinary or non-disciplinary action as the IDFPR may deem proper with regard to the registration of any person issued under the Law to operate a dispensing organization or act as a dispensing organization agent, including imposing fines not to exceed $10,000 for each violation, for any violations under the Law and rules adopted in accordance therewith. All final administrative decisions of the IDFPR are subject to judicial review under the Administrative Review Law and its rules [410 ILCS 130/155]. The term "administrative decision" is defined as in Section 3-101 of the Code of Civil Procedure [410 ILCS 130/130(n)].

**EDUCATION LAW**

**6-100. Can a university, college or other post-secondary educational institution restrict the use of medical marijuana?**

Yes. A university, college, or other post-secondary educational institution has the right to restrict or prohibit the use of medical marijuana on its property. [410 ILCS 130/30(h)]

**6-101. Can a school refuse to enroll or penalize a person for holding the status as a medical marijuana user?**

No. A school is prohibited from refusing to enroll or penalize a person for holding the status as a medical marijuana user, *unless* failing to do so would place the school in violation of federal law or put it in jeopardy of losing a monetary or licensing-related benefit under a federal law or rule. [410 ILCS 130/40(a)(1)]

**VIOLATION / SUSPENSION / REVOCATIONS OF REGISTRATION**

**7-100. My cultivation center was found in violation under the Act – What consequences may I be facing?**

The IDA or IDPH may suspend or revoke a cultivation center's registration granted under Illinois' Medical Marijuana Law for violations [410 ILCS 130/110(a) and 410 ILCS 130/185(a)]. All administrative hearings under the Act are conducted in accordance with the IDPH's rules governing administrative hearings [410 ILCS 130/175]. A suspension or revocation is seemed a final Agency Action subject to judicial review by the Illinois Circuit Court [410 ILCS 130/155, 410 ILCS 130/110(b), and 410 ILCS 130/185(b)].

### 7-101. My dispensing organization was found in violation under the Act – What consequences may I be facing?

Notwithstanding any other criminal penalties related to the unlawful possession of cannabis, the IDFPR or IDPH may revoke, suspend, place on probation, reprimand, refuse to issue or renew, or take any other disciplinary or non-disciplinary action as the IDFPR may deem proper with regard to the registration of any person issued under the Law to operate a dispensing organization or act as a dispensing organization agent, including imposing fines not to exceed $10,000 for each violation, for any violations under the Law and rules adopted in accordance therewith [410 ILCS 130/130(n) and 410 ILCS 130/185(a)]. All final administrative decisions of the IDFPR are subject to judicial review under the Administrative Review Law and its rules [410 ILCS 130/155 and 410 ILCS 130/185(b)]. The term "administrative decision" is defined as in Section 3-101 of the Code of Civil Procedure [410 ILCS 130/130(n)].

## CRIMINAL LAW

### 8-100. Other than the presentation of my registry identification card, will law enforcement know that I am legally authorized to use medical marijuana if I don't have my card on me?

First, a registered qualifying patient or designated caregiver must keep their registry identification card in his or her possession at all times when engaging in the medical use of cannabis [410 ILCS 130/70(a)]. When a patient is approved a registry identification card for medical marijuana use, the IDPH forwards the approved patients registration number to the Illinois Secretary of State where by a notation is made on the patient's driving record for law enforcement purposes. Similarly, the IDPH will notify the Illinois Secretary of State of the patient no longer holds a valid registry card. [410 ILCS 130/60(d)]

### 8-101. What happens if I am a registered patient and the police find more than the 2.5 ounce amount in my possession?

The Police may seize the amounts exceeding the amounts allowed under the Act. [410 ILCS 130/25(l)].

### 8-102. Does a registration ID card or certificate (or application thereof) give the police reasonable suspicion or probable cause to search a person, home or property?

No, the possession of a registration card or certificate (or application thereof) does not constitute reasonable suspicion or probable cause to allow the police to perform a search. However, if probable cause exists on other grounds, such registration or certificate does not preclude the existence of probable cause. [410 ILCS 130/25(l)]

### 8-103. Can I be arrested or prosecuted for being in the presence of a registered marijuana user or assisting a medical marijuana patient with the Act of administering cannabis?

No, so long as the user has a valid registry card. If the registration card is expired, you may be at risk. [410 ILCS 130/25(f)]

### 8-104. Are there places where medical marijuana cannot be used or possessed under the Law?

Medical marijuana cannot be *possessed* in: (a) a school bus [410 ILCS 130/30(a)(2)(A)]; (b) on school grounds of any primary or secondary school [410 ILCS 130/30(a)(2)(B)]; (c) correctional facility [410 ILCS 130/30(a)(2)(C)]; (d) by a driver or passenger in a vehicle on any Illinois highway unless in a sealed, tamper-evident container [410 ILCS 130/30(a)(2)(D) ) and 625 ILCS 5/11-502.1(b) and (c)]; (e) in a vehicle not open to the public which is not reasonably secured, sealed, or in a tamper-evident container, AND reasonably inaccessible while the vehicle is moving [410 ILCS 130/30(a)(2)(E)]; and (f) a private residence used as a licensed child care or other similar social service care [410 ILCS 130/30(a)(2)(F)].

Medical marijuana cannot be *used* : (a) in a school bus [410 ILCS 130/30(a)(3)(A)]; (b) on school grounds of any primary or secondary school [410 ILCS 130/30(a)(3)(B)]; (c) correctional facility [410 ILCS 130/30(a)(3)(C)]; (d) in a motor vehicle, aircraft, or motor boat [410 ILCS 130/30(a)(3)(D) and 30(a)(3)(5); 625 ILCS 5/11-502.1(a)]; (e) a private residence used as a licensed child care, foster care, or other similar social service care

[410 ILCS 130/30(a)(3)(E)]; (f) a public place where an individual could reasonably be expected to be observed by others, or where smoking is prohibited under the Smoke Free Illinois Act (including places leased or owned by a unit of government [410 ILCS 130/30(a)(4)]; (g) in close proximity of a person under age 18 [410 ILCS 130/30(a)(3)(G)].

## 8-105. What is the criminal penalty for violating the Illinois Motor Vehicle/Medical Marijuana laws related to illegal possession or use of medical marijuana?

A violation of possession or use of medical marijuana is a Class A misdemeanor and is subject to revocation of his or her medical cannabis card for a period of 2 years from the end of the sentence imposed and, where applicable, shall be subject to revocation of his or her status as a medical cannabis caregiver, medical cannabis cultivation center agent, or medical cannabis dispensing organization agent for a period of 2 years from the end of the sentence imposed [625 ILCS 5/11-502.1(d)(1)-(4)].

## 8-106. Can a registered patient that drives be arrested for being under the influence of medical marijuana?

Yes. A registered qualifying patient can be arrested or prosecuted for reckless driving or driving under the influence of cannabis where probable cause exists. [410 ILCS 130/30(b)]

## 8-107. What is the penalty for misrepresenting to law enforcement that use or possession of marijuana for medicinal purposes in an effort to avoid arrest or prosecution?

Under the Medical Marijuana Law, this is a petty offence punishable up to a fine up to $1,000, plus any other penalties that may apply for making false statement or for use of cannabis other than use under the Act. [410 ILCS 130/30(c)]

## 8-108. What is the penalty for misrepresenting or fraudulently supplying material misinformation of a medical condition to a physician in an effort to obtain a written certification?

Under the Medical Marijuana Law, this is a petty offence punishable up to a fine up to $1,000, plus any other criminal penalties that may apply for related to the unlawful possession of cannabis. [410 ILCS 130/30(d)]

**8-109. What is the consequence of a registered cardholder or caregiver unlawfully selling medical marijuana?**

The registry identification card of the offending cardholder or caregiver will have his or her card revoked. [410 ILCS 130/30(e)]

**8-110. What is the consequence of a registered cardholder or caregiver refusing to take a field sobriety test for operating a vehicle under the influence of cannabis?**

The offender commits a Class A misdemeanor and the registry identification card of the offending cardholder or caregiver will have his or her card revoked for a period of 2 years from the end of any imposed sentence for violating the law regarding the unlawful use or possession of medical cannabis in a motor vehicle (625 ILCS 5/11-502.1) . [410 ILCS 130/30(f)]

**8-111. I was convicted of a crime in my past – Am I automatically disqualified from being approved a registration to own and operate a cultivation center in Illinois?**

Most misdemeanors will not serve as an automatic bar to an applicant applying for registration as a cultivation center. However, most felony convictions will bar an applicant. An application for a cultivation center permit *must* be denied by the IDA if: (i) one or more of the prospective principal officers or board members has been convicted of an "excluded offense" [410 ILCS 130/85(e)(3)(e.g., a violent crime, violation of a controlled substance law that is categorized as a felony – unless such felony is related to certain offenses related to reasonable amounts if medical marijuana and is waived by the reviewing Department [410 ILCS 130/10(l)]); (ii) a principal officer or board member of the cultivation center has been convicted of a felony under any federal or state law [410 ILCS 130/85(e)(6); or (iii) a principal officer or board member of the cultivation center has been convicted of any violation of Article 28 of the Criminal Code of 2012 (criminal offenses related to illegal gambling in Illinois), or substantially similar laws of any other jurisdiction [410 ILCS 130/85(e)(7).

**8-112. What criminal consequences does an IDPH, IDA, IDFPR or any other State agency or local government employee for unlawfully disclosing private patient, designated caregiver, cultivation center, or dispensing organization information under the Act?**

It is a Class B misdemeanor with a $1,000 fine for any person, including an employee or official of the IDPH, IDA, IDFPR or another State agency or local government, to breach the confidentiality of information obtained under this Act [410 ILCS 130/145(c)].

**8-113. Can federal law enforcement arrest or charge me for using, selling, or cultivating medical marijuana under the protections provided for under the Illinois Medical Marijuana Law?**

Yes, but it is unlikely based on the federal government's historic inaction against other jurisdictions with similar medical marijuana laws. Since cannabis remains listed as an illegal controlled substance under federal law and there is no equivalent federal law that recognizes and affords protections for the lawful use of marijuana for medicinal purposes, it is possible that federal law enforcement could charge/arrest a registered patient, dispensary, or cultivation center with violating applicable federal criminal laws prohibiting the use, sale, manufacture, or possession of marijuana. However, the federal government has generally recognized and respected each state's sovereign right to exercise its own police powers to regulate legal and/or illegal use, possession, sale, and manufacture of controlled substances within its own state boundaries and its citizens.

**PROFESSIONAL DISCIPLINARY ACTION**

**9-100. Can I be subject to disciplinary action for being in the physical presence of a registered marijuana patient or assisting a marijuana patient with the act of administering cannabis?**

No, so long as the patient has a valid registry card. If the registration card is expired, you may be at risk. [410 ILCS 130/25(f)]

**9-101. What disciplinary action will a physician face for violating any of the certification compliance restrictions or regulations?**

The IDPH can report a physician to the IDFPR so long as it has reasonable cause to show that a violation was committed [410 ILCS 130/35(c)], and a violation is a violation of the Medical Practice Act of 1987 [410 ILCS 130/35(d)].

**9-102. Can I be disciplined (and arrested) by my occupational or professional licensing board for medical use of marijuana under the Act or serving a registered caregiver to a medical marijuana patient?**

A registered qualifying patient *cannot* be subject to civil penalty or disciplinary action by an occupational or professional licensing board, for the medical use of cannabis under the Act if: (1) it does not exceed the "adequate supply" of 2.5 ounces; AND (2) it does not impair the licensed professional when he or she is engaged in the practice of his or her profession [410 ILCS 130/25(a)]; (3) it does not constitute negligence, professional malpractice, or professional misconduct [410 ILCS 130/30(a)(1)]; or (4) for possession of cannabis that is incidental to medical use, but is not usable cannabis as defined in the Law [410 ILCS 130/25(c)].

A registered designated caregiver is not subject to disciplinary action by an occupational or professional licensing board, for acting in accordance with the Law to assist a registered qualifying patient to whom he or she is connected through the Department's registration process with the medical use of cannabis: (1) and the designated caregiver possesses an amount of cannabis that does not exceed the 2.5 ounce adequate supply of usable cannabis [410 ILCS 130/30(a)(2)]; or (2) if the possession of cannabis that is incidental to medical use, is not usable cannabis as defined in the Law [410 ILCS 130/25(c)].

## LANDLORD –TENANT LAW

### 10-100. Can a Landlord prohibit a tenant and any visitor from smoking medical marijuana on a leased premises?

Yes. Landlords have the right to prohibit the smoking of cannabis on the lease premises. [410 ILCS 130/40(a)(1)] A landlord will not be in violation of the American with Disabilities Act for prohibiting the medical use of marijuana on its premises since federal law does not recognize the lawful use of medical marijuana.

## CIVIL RIGHTS / CONCERNED CITIZENS

### 11-100. Can a registered user be denied or disqualified from needed medical care?

No. A registered user that uses medical marijuana is not deemed to be using an "illicit drug," and therefore, he or she cannot be denied or disqualified from needed medical care including, for example, organ transplants. [410 ILCS 130/40(a)(2)]

### 11-101. Is any property owner, person, or business establishment required to make accommodations for, or allow use of, medical marijuana?

No. No person or establishment in lawful possession or ownership of property is required to make accommodations for or allow the use of medical marijuana. [410 ILCS 130/40(e)]

**11-102. I believe a cultivation center is creating public health hazards – what can I do?**

If you have a reasonable belief that a cultivation center's cannabis-infused product poses a public health hazard, you can refer the cultivation center to the IDPH, or contact a local health organization who, in turn, may refer the cultivation center to the IDPH. If the IDPH finds that a cannabis-infused product poses a health hazard, it may without administrative procedure to bond, bring an action for immediate injunctive relief to require that action be taken as the court may deem necessary to meet the hazard of the cultivation center [410 ILCS 130/80(c)].

**11-103. Do the Illinois State Police, the IDFPR, and/or IDPH have a right to inspect my registered cultivation center or dispensing organization facility in spite of the fact that I am strictly complying with all the rules and regulations required under the Law?**

Yes. Dispensing organizations and cultivations centers are subject to random inspection and marijuana testing by the IDFPR, IDPH, and Illinois State Police [410 ILCS 130/130(o), 410 ILCS 130/105(h) and (i), and 410 ILCS 130/80(b)]. The IDPH may at all times enter every building, room, basement, enclosure, or premises occupied or used or suspected of being occupied or used for the production, preparation, manufacture for sale, storage, sale, distribution or transportation of medical cannabis edible products, to inspect the premises and all utensils, fixtures, furniture, and machinery used for the preparation of these products [410 ILCS 130/80(b)].

**11-104. I am concerned about my privacy and the information I disclose to the IDPH, PDA, IDFRP, and Illinois State Police as a patient, designated caregiver, or related to my interest in a cultivation center or dispensing organization – Is this information confidential or protected?**

Subject to the privacy/confidentiality exceptions provided below, the following information received and records kept by the IDPH, PDA, IDFRP, and Illinois State Police are subject to all applicable federal privacy laws, confidential, and exempt from the Freedom of Information Act (e.g., FOIA requests), and not subject to disclosure to any individual or public or private entity, except as necessary for authorized employees of those authorized agencies (amongst one another) to perform official duties under the

Act: (i) Applications and renewals, their contents, and supporting information submitted by qualifying patients and designated caregivers, including information regarding their designated caregivers and physicians; (ii) Applications and renewals, their contents, and supporting information submitted by or on behalf of cultivation centers and dispensing organizations in compliance with the Act, including their physical addresses; (iii) The individual names and other information identifying persons to whom the IDPH has issued registry ID cards; (iv) Any dispensing information required to be kept under Section 135 (change in designated dispensing organization), Section 150 (registry identification and registration certificate verification), or IDPH, IDA, or IDFPR rules shall identify cardholders and registered cultivation centers by their registry identification numbers and medical marijuana dispensing organizations by their registration number and not contain names or other personally identifying information; and (v) All medical records provided to the IDPH in connection with an application for a registry card [410 ILCS 130/145(a)(1) – (5) and 410 ILCS 130/150(a)].

Exceptions to the privacy and confidentiality of information provided under the Act include: (i) IDPH, IDA, or IDFPR employees may notify law enforcement about falsified or fraudulent information submitted to the Departments if the employee who suspects that falsified or fraudulent information has been submitted conferred with his or her supervisor and both agree that circumstances exist that warrant reporting; (ii) If the employee conferred with his or her supervisor and both agree that circumstances exist that warrant reporting, IDPH employees may notify the IDFRP if there is reasonable cause to believe a physician: (a) issued a written certification without a bona fide physician-patient relationship under this Act, (b) issued a written certification to a person who was not under the physician's care for the debilitating medical condition, or (c) failed to abide by the acceptable and prevailing standard of care when evaluating a patient's medical condition; (iii) The IDPH, IDA, or IDFPR may notify State or local law enforcement about apparent criminal violations of the Act if the employee who suspects the offense has conferred with his or her supervisor and both agree that circumstances exist that warrant reporting; (iv) medical marijuana cultivation center agents and medical marijuana dispensing organizations may notify the IDPH, IDA, or IDFPR of a suspected violation or attempted violation of the Act or the rules issued under it; (v) Each Department may verify registry identification cards under Section 150 (registry identification and registration certification verification); and (vi) The submission of the report to the General Assembly under Section 160 (annual reports) [410 ILCS 130/145(b)(1) – (6)].

# FAMILY LAW

**12-100. Can a parent be denied a right to custody or visitation if he or she is a registered medical marijuana user?**

A parent otherwise entitled to custody of or visitation or parenting time with a minor may not be denied that right because he or she is a registered user. There is no presumption of neglect or child endangerment unless there is clear and convincing evidence the parent's actions in relation to marijuana use are such that they created an unreasonable danger to the safety of the minor [410 ILCS 130/40(b)]. Remember, medical marijuana cannot be used in close proximity of a person under age 18 [410 ILCS 130/30(a)(3)(G)].

www.ingramcontent.com/pod-product-compliance
Lightning Source LLC
Chambersburg PA
CBHW070715180526
45167CB00004B/1482